salmonpoetry

Publishing Irish & International

Poetry Since 1981

Salmon Poetry gratefully acknowledges the support of
The Arts Council / An Chomhairle Ealaíon

Flight Paths Over Finglas
Rachael Hegarty

First published in 2017 by Salmon Poetry
Reprinted in 2018 by Salmon Poetry
Cliffs of Moher, County Clare, Ireland
Website: www.salmonpoetry.com
Email: info@salmonpoetry.com

ISBN 978-1-910669-93-8

COVER IMAGE: © *Christos Georghiou | Dreamstime.com*
COVER DESIGN & TYPESETTING: *Siobhán Hutson*
Printed in Ireland by Sprint Print

For my family, our friends and Finglas

Acknowledgements

A big thank you to all the mentor-poets who helped this poet to poem –
Paula Meehan, Sinéad Morrissey, Siobhan Daffy, Dermot Bolger, Aidan
Mathews, Theo Dorgan, Ciaran Carson, Brendan Kennelly, Gerry Dawe,
Eavan Boland, Eiléan Ní Chuilleanáin, Erica Meitner, Tess Taylor, Tom O'
Grady, Jessie Lendennie; the poet-academics – Antoinette Quinn, Nicky
Grene and Michael Pierse; my gifted classmate-poets at the Seamus Heaney
Centre and the Oscar Wilde Centre; the songsters and the ghost-poets,
especially Seamus Heaney and Maya Angelou.

I am much obligated to my workmates and gaffers at the Trinity Access
Programme and CDETB for their encouragement, sense of fun while earn-
ing mon and timetabling patience.

Hats off to my students: ye are my best teachers ever.

I am indebted to the staff at the Tyrone Guthrie Centre for their delightful
creation station up there, by a lake in Monaghan.

This collection would not have been possible without the love and cheer-
leading of my family and friends or the passionate faith of Karl Quinn.

Some of these poems, or versions of these poems, appeared in *Poetry Ireland
Review, Cyphers, Southword, Orbis, The SHOp, Our Shared Japan, Fire, The
Stony Thursday Book, Crannóg Magazine* and *The Irish Traveller Voice*.

Finally, fair play to Jessie Lendennie and Siobhán Hutson at Salmon Poetry
– they are waking the feminists in the Irish Poetry world.

Contents

Migratory Birds

Mating

Working Birds

Epilogue

You're in the back cul-de-sac with street pals and games:
stuck-in-the-mud, kick-the-can, red-rover or Cowboys
and Indians. You — you're always with the Indians.

If you leave Finglas, venture past the River Tolka,
you have to stay together and hold hands. You sing:

Everywhere we go, people always ask us, who are ya?
Where deya come from? We're from Finglas, mighty mighty Finglas.

Above, Them Before

Ripples

I

Rank, Profession or Occupation: *House Duties*

Nanny called herself the Snobs' Charwoman,
Premier Potwalloper, Scullery Savant, the Duchess of Dusting,
    a Baking Beauty and the Silver Horde Sheener.
Swollen ankles, stone-sore knees, her hands chaffed vermilion
        as she shovelled out ash from blackened hearths.
She was forced to earn a shillin' by scrubbing out blood, sweat and snot
        from bed linen, hankies and rich strangers' underwear.

There are things a death cert can't tell you.
Early every morning she'd kiss her four sleeping kids to quell
    her fear of the Cruelty Man taking them away
to Goldenbridge. She'd set out a breakfast of milk and rye bread,
        apples and boiled eggs for school lunches, leave
a coddle of pearl barley and crubeens cooking on the glimmer.

II

Date of Death: *14th of February 1965*
Sex: *Female*
Condition: *Widow*
Age: *65 Years*

She used to light candles at Whitefriar's
where Saint Valentine's relics rest, way west of Rome.
She'd nip in, pay the ha'penny,
bow her head and tell the patron saint of love to send word
to her husband in heaven.
She lilted a litany of Hail Marys for her well-fed schoolchildren.
Incense drifted in the air,
parishioners tip-toed, a Carmelite minded silence and stared.

They say Valentine gave a yellow crocus
to the blind daughter of his jailer. The girl regained her sight.
Surely, the sky opened the day my Nanny died.
On canal bank walk – a miraculous shower of early golden croci,
aureate from heaven, petal cups of covenant –
her husband sent back a sign. Blossoms down the water line.

III

Certified Cause of Death and Duration of Illness: *Asphyxiation*
from drowning in the Grand Canal at Basin Lane on that date.
The occurrence was accidental.

She knows the canal is man-made
and knows the names of birds, migrants from the tidal rivers:
    mute swans, mallards and water hens
nest past the towpath, secreted in rushes, at the water's edge.
    There's a heron near the lock gates.
He swoops down, seems to play with the gush and eddy of the weir,
    dive-bombs into the cold navy blue
only to re-emerge with a fat grey speckled pike for his tea.

Nanny sits beneath a weeping birch
and imagines below the surface: aquatic life, the silky mud, gentle silt.
    If she could swim, she'd swim down beneath
the clamour of a city, the din of the flats and the ruckus of a big family.
    She could immerse her whole tired body,
glide through thread leaves and savour the near silence of underwater.

IV

Signature, *Qualification and Residence of Informant: Certificate received from Dr. John P. Stanley, Coroner for the City of Dublin, Inquest held the 26th of February 1965.*

Even gravediggers hate the thoughts of a night burial.
There's no give. The clay needs at least half a day of sunshine
     to allow for the bite of spade and shovel of soil.
Then there's the dark, folks walking into headstones, stumbling,
     wishing someone had remembered a torch.
The icy mid-February night air would set the priest's rattling off
     a bit of a prayer before fleeing a family plot.

My Nanny got lucky. A stranger told a kind lie.
They buried her in the afternoon, in the sunny cold and spring light,
     laid to rest beside her husband and them before.
Her children, grandchildren, all the old neighbours from the Liberties
     gathered by her graveside. Her unborn granddaughter
plunked a snowdrop; let it fall, like a last whisper at the coffin lid.

Night Watchman Photograph, 1948

In darkness, you Grandda, kept nix from a photo-frame world.
Your tired smile lingered on your sleeping family's doubt
over a day's work, the gaffer's shout or a teacher's clout.
The night sky helped. The plough and the stars unfurled.
By day your chislers yearned to sit into your lap, cosy-curled,
or wanted a chase from the man with the fee-fi-fo-fum mouth,
until the fun ended with one of your blue-lipped coughing bouts.
Outside the flat, oak leaves gale-fluttered and steady-whorled.

Nanny dreamed the length of you beside her, one-armed and lanky.
She'd not mind the scourge of a cough, the sheets slack with fever,
the soppin' snot rags you tried to hide in a badly fitted prosthetic fist
or the wild garlic she steeped in the tea, that made you smell manky.
She'd endure everything, anything, as long as you didn't leave her.
Factory days mangled you. You downed tools and watched night shift.

Costume Barracks

The Boston nieces and nephews call this one a very Irish love story.
      Granny Mary was born in a British barracks
of limestone block, timber doors, fanlight, rendered chimney stacks
      and cast iron gutters for Athlone's streams of rain.
Daughter of a Royal Army Lieutenant, she could say nothing
      to the shoe-polishing-nutter about a stonemason's lad she'd met.
by Magazine Gate. They courted beyond the town's walls,
      the streets' gawkers and spiteful talkers.
A wander by the River Shannon could make a body fall in love,
      a July swim would have you near drowned in lust
but a man who could name all the wild flowers on a sunny riverbank –
      birdsfoot, rush, water avens, ox-eyed daisy and cowslip –
he's the one who'd have you on the run with n'er a backward glance,
      to take a chance on mucked-up boots and unknown roads.
They learned the names of Dublin's flowering weeds – pansy, poppy
      and the odd snap dragon. Blooms thrived from cracks in paths,
out of auld mortar and midst broken bits of granite, sandstone and redbrick.

Ancient Guild of Incorporated Brick and Stonelayers

I show your great-grandson the union card
and he says *it's tattered but cool, really cool.*
Stonelayer is what he reads in his geology book.
For him you are knee deep in soil and muck,
happily diggin' and pitchin' the stone line,
a dark subsurface, the biomantle underlayer
of igneous, sedimentary and metamorphic rock.
He wants to know more about this ancient guild
that sanctioned the making of brick from gravel,
clays flecked with quartz or mica, snail shells,
auld animal bones and human artifacts. *Ancient
Guild of Incorporated Brick*: he shifts the phrase
around his head and lips to see a band of builder
brothers, crusaders milling a field for breezeblocks.

How do I tell our eldest the bricklayer never got
to build his own home? The Lockout blacklist meant
Grandda endured a rented, musty-roomed damp cottage –
scullery, outside privy, and seven kids squabbling
for their share of space in two second-hand double beds.
Icy nights and the coal scuttle low, the folks piled coats,
sacks, hearth rugs, backdoor mats, to try and warm
the croupy children's spindly-hungry bones.
Our son needs to learn guild brickies saved our kin.
I read out the best bit: *Building Workers' Trade Union.*
Me eldest is pre-teen lit. *It's alright Ma, I know –
strike pay, food parcels, guild coal causa no dole.*
He's on his feet, the stonemason's flesh and blood
holds a union card up: *kicking ass for the working class.*

Her X Mark

Her small, neat x mark
is all we have left.
Maternal death's as dark
as a young family's bereft.
Greatnana bled out
on a bed of sack and hay.
No rage, no roars, no shout,
just a brief milky stay.
She crooked her last infant,
gave of the breast,
life-love-death, an instant
in whispered breaths.
But Catherine Allen Kilkenny was here.
Her x mark. A kiss. The heart's spear.

The Receipt

All we have now is an old square of flittered paper
with the details from an undertaker's on Parnell Street.
The company name, in fancy calligraphy. A by-line —
funeral requisites of every description stocked — puzzles me.
The date in March, the record of an infant's D.O.B. & D.O.D.
The purchase price, £2, a currency as long gone as …

But it's my father's penmanship, soft black strokes
at an odd slant. *A child s coffin*. He forgot the apostrophe.
Or maybe he just couldn't write it down, cruel pen on paper —
the ownership, the relationship between his child and a coffin.
My mother gave us all a laminated photocopy of the receipt:
the filigreed evidence of the newborn boy she never nursed,
a child no priest would bless. Proof of the tiny white coffin
our father had to bury, by himself, at night in the angel plot.

International Judo Federation Referee Identification

Mí na Marbh, month of the dead, and I hold his memory in my hand.
  I flick-weave his judo referee card in and out of my fingers.

Once more, we're lined up, lying bolt-still, on patched judo mats,
  in canvas judoji and lulled by the smell of sibling sweat.
Training's over, bows done and the Da is about to do his trick
  of run, leap, shoulder-roll and fly over his nine kids.
We count him down – three, two, one. We hear his rapid feet.
  He's over us, mid-air, the ten-hour-day van man: all there.

Autumns, he'd take us *November walking to hear the dead talking*.
Leaves of amber oaks, rusty yews, tawny chestnuts and flaming ash.
  He'd say we could eat and live off the colours in the Phoenix Park.

Hatchlings

The Song Map

Late at night, we hear folks sing of women, a *weile, weile, waile*,
Of jailed men: demented with the jingle-jangle of an auld triangle.
Da belts out his dream of Joe Hill. Ma keens over *The Foggy Dew*.

We learn the song map of our island via landmarks of mangled hearts.
Intown: *On Raglan Road*; out the country: *Down by the Sally Gardens*.
Lovely bockety words, feral jigs and lonely airs haunt our heads.

We are lulled, fall asleep, top-and-tail siblings in a rickety bunk bed.

Chasing Chiselers

We all hide under the stairs. Pushing each other further
into the crawl space. Four sets of little elbows and feet
poke one another and shove for room. We whist. And whist.

He cracks open the hall door, sniff-snuffling the air.

Fee-fi-fo-fum, I smell a load of chiselers wantin' fun.

There's a scatter.

Two kids swing out of each of his arms,

spin and swim,
nose out
the doughy-scents
of the bread man's
clocking-off.

The Bonesetter

Banjaxed men arrive at our house, at all hours, in all states.
Our father meets them with nothing but a nod of the head.

The patient lies on the kitchen table. Da's hands steeple,
soaked in poteen to thwack heat into skin, flesh and blades of bone.
Da raises an arm, hauls the aching shoulder back into place.
There's a distinctive click, the sudden shift and shudder.

A mended man sits right up. Aul'fellas share a drop of the hard stuff.

Run, Ma, Run

17.05.1974 Talbot Street

A rainfall
   of window
      shards

         zOOm.

Ma throws daughter
         upon son.

                     Pram-run.

                        Shopping bags   agape,

bricks,
mortar,
blocks
tattered.

People, legs, arms   shattered.

                              Kids' faces, blood-battered.

Garda. *ANOTHER BOMB.*

28

shoulders Ma.

Pram veers.

Grab brother.

Somewhere, a ni-naw.

Sobs suck-choke craw.

Run. Big-Belly Ma.

Save daughter.

Save son.

Where's me Da?

Ma

Run

Run

An aulwan

29

Fried Bread

Hunger's no game. But her robbin' thrills me to bits.
She palms sweets from Cronin's shop
and pinches apples outta Whelan's garden.

One day she swipes her own Da's fried bread.
It's scalding hot. Rasher fat still sizzles on the crust. I watch her toss
the slice from hand to hand to cool it down.
She tears into it like a mangy dog at the black bags on bin day.

I don't bagsie her ends. I never eat fried bread.

Child of The Emergency

Da cleaves bone and sinew
from roast chickens.

Strips onions. Crushes garlic. Adds
all to his stockpot of potato peelings
broccoli stalks and carnip tops.

Nine kids savour dinner.
Sunday's kitchen simmers.

Scallywaggin'

Between the Tolka and a disused quarry we learn
to cook a soup of puddle water and dandelions.
We brew it in a discarded tin of council paint
and stir it with windfall bits of twigs. Sticks

double as daggers. The longer ones are Finglas swords
pulled from the belt loops of corduroy scabbards.
Warrior Queens-in-training, we batter unseen enemies.

Nestlings

Tide Pools, Donabate

I mosey past the waterline of seaweed and plastic rubbish.
Run, spring, boost a big goosh, up onto the rocks. *Mind yourself,*
mind the jags don't snag you. Don't be running back with scrawbs.
Some of the bigger rocks make me go on hunkers. Breath in gob,
I have to crawl: hand-foot, hand-foot, hand-foot. I learn
to lean into leaps, scramble, tumble and steady me jelly-legs.
A seagull and me wait to hear the plop of rock into a tide pool,
peer into sways of sea-weed, a sandy bed. Try grab a hermit-crab.
I look back and see me folks sitting behind a windbreaker,
basking in gleams of mica stones from the Martello Tower.
Sit down, stretch out on the flat of a baking-warm brown rock.
If I close my eyes, lashes-tipping, the whole world is a pale orange.
Hear the rush and hush of the waves. Rush and hush. Rush. Hush.
Everything that ever was, is and will be, smells of the sea.

Communion

She yards out chiffon and sorts the paper pattern for me frock.
The kitchen table's a feast of pins, shears and tailor's chalk.
Ma steadies and measures me. She cuts the pattern on the bias.
Watch her thread the bobbin with pursed lips, a sleight of hand
and a careful lean into the machine. I'm lulled by her tap dance
on the floor pedal and how her swift hands and gymnastic fingers
feed material under the hammering needle and steely Singer's foot.
Ma keeps her head down but explains the work as she goes along.

French seam, a double security for a tree-shinny-tom-boy like you,
appliqué of ribbon on cuffs to save delicate sleeves from pure filth,
a white feather trim, like Noah's resting dove, warm at your neck,
the lining of linen to keep you cool if the Child of Prague glows,
a blind hem and waist darts with give for growth. Lemme fit you.
She zips, buttons and ribbons the white dress: *a smashin' beauty.*

Mrs. Murphy

The odd time there's a sighting of Mrs. M, head down,
scrubbing out their front porch with a hard bristle brush.
Crimson knuckled, elbow grease, arms reach, going ninety.
A bucket of rinse water. She starts off again. Back into it.

You wonder about the invisible dirt plaguing her doorstep.
One Saturday you see her washing windows. Spy her pale
pink basin of sudsy water and twists of scrunched newspapers
from a hideout behind their garden wall. She says nothing.

Her eyes swollen purple, a gashed brow. Her hands shake.
You leg it, race the street shadows to your front gate,
clutch cold wrought iron in your fists. Wish you could ice
her black eye, Dettol and plaster that gash. Mrs. M needs

to see the state of your gaff: its manky porch and pawed windows.
She should have a quiet word with your Ma and her sisters.

Being Bold at the Dunsink Observatory

It's easy to be bold in an observatory.
All you have to do is find the stairs.
Each step up into the dark tingles
a cold excitement on the back of the neck.
Every creak on wood is a suppressed breath.
You come to a huge mahogany door, turn
a brass knob and walk into a domed room.
You look up, gobsmacked by a revolving roof.
The sky, the massive sky, wide-open to you.

The slip of a new moon and one low, lone star.
Venus shines down on the darkest corner of Finglas.

Mamó Mór

Meself and mock-penance stand in the middle of our kitchen floor.
Me hair is matted with muck, mud streelled, new jeans, torn knees.
I've been playing with the bold boys in the back fields.
Auntie Kathleen downs tonic wine and laughs out loud.

My mother, hand on hip, gawks at me with deadeners in her eyes.
Oh you're of your Mamó Mór's ilk alright, only happy outside,
wandering roads, haring 'neath hedges and lighting bonfires with wans
from that halting site. She'll never be dead, as long as you live.

Steam hisses out from between the iron and board. Women talk different
when housekeeping so I fold teatowels and press the Ma to tell more
about the woman whose mouth could slag a body to bits. They say I hailed
out of her very spit. *Kind to kin but slámóg-rough, like a Traveller woman.*

My aunt stands up, clasps my wrist and looks at me, eye to eye –
Like a traveller woman, my foot, your Mamó Mór was a traveller woman.

The Witch Sniffer

The welfare man's a sleveen of a witch sniffer. I must smell
right if I've any chance of getting through the inquisition
for a School Clothing, Footwear and Book Allowance.
You're not going up to that place smelling of petunia oils
and looking like Janis Joplin off out to the gig at Woodstock.
Ma smears lemon rind and juice on me wrists and sprinkles
drops of vanilla essence all over me second-best dress and jacket.
The witch sniffer has a grá for girls who do little but bake and skivvy.
Ma removes me bangles, beads, bauble earrings and granny's brooch.
The heart of the Claddagh ring stares up at me in shock.
She whips off the PLO scarf, zips me jacket, all the way, to the neck
and coils up me tailing-long red hair under a grey woollen hat.
Ma flattens it down, fits the cap snug. She bites at the fat of her lip:
don't look him in the eye, don't let that witch sniffer come near you.

Bareback Riding in Finglas South

There is a knack
when you go bareback,
riding a stolen pony
to stop you feeling lonely.

You wait until after dark
to begin this solo lark.
You take a length of rope,
a sweet red apple and hope

the chestnut racer stands by the hedge.
The council wall becomes a mounting ledge.
Like Eve, you put the apple to his mouth,
with hemp for reins, you amble south.

By the riverbank, you dig heels into his flank –
a nicker and you bolt out of the ordinary.

Fledglings

Broadcast

Ma stares at the radio.
She stops peeling the spuds.

His family kept vigil. A waterbed protected his fragile bones.

Our Ma sighs and walks out the kitchen door.
She grabs a tin bin lid from the stunned backyard.

West Belfast women bang dustbin lids to alert others of the news.

Some aulwans from our estate are out the front. Hunkered
down on the footpaths and belting the life out of their own bin lids.

In Belfast they have built barricades, hijacked and burned out cars.

Down our way, the lads with oxblood Docs, kick the Jaysus
outta steel shutters. Bash. Thud-n-Rattle. Bash. Thud-n-Rattle.

After 66 days of hunger strike …

Ma and other mothers bash and clatter tin bin lids.
Starlings take fright and scatter off the roof of the Blacker.

Grizzly

Bear with me

is what the Ma says
as she hauls another load
in from the washing line.

The daughter's a slow learner
of the sheet-folding-dance-steps
with Our Lady of Perpetual Laundry.

Bear with me.

The Da shows her the foundations'
deep trickery as they lay red brick
next to sturdier breeze blocks.

They build a wall high enough
to keep the piebald ponies out
and the younger kids in the garden.

Bear with me.

Her parents work and work.
She lies in wait
for a grizzly bear.

He prowls near the side hedge.
She batters him to bits. Then
feeds him to the dogs in the street.

Next morning, she makes
tea and toast. Brings her folks
breakfast in bed.

Horse Fair

My brothers are enchanted by ponies.
One after another, I name
as many as I can remember:

Connemara, Piebald, Kerry Bog,
Irish Draught, a white light racer
and the blackest black Irish Hunter.

The horses trot into Smithfield,
led by Travellers, reins and bit.
Heads high as the Walking People's sky.

I pull my palm over the tongue and groove
of a yellow barrel wagon of ash wood.
Breathe for the scent of windfall fires,

take in the small door, a raised bed,
and tell the little brothers
Mamó Mór might have lived in one like this.

A man steps out from behind a horse and asks
Was she a Carroll? I nod my yes.
The Traveller says: *You're every bar of a Carroll.*

Tuesdays in Ballymun

for Sinéad Morrissey

We meet on Tuesdays at the Tech. It's always night, classes in darkness, all quiet in the locked school yard.
Don't know what to be saying; I trace his guitar-callused hands, he taps on me pen-bet thumb and fingertip.

During the Siege of Leningrad,
Akhmatova saw Russian women
defend homes with boat hooks
as she ran to Shostakovich's flat.

Ballymon: Dublin's old plough lands. 7 15-storey towers, 6 4-storey buildings and 19 8-storey blocks.
No front or back gardens — 3,000 families doing the do and living out their lives on top of each other.

A door flung open — widened
to the strains of piano keys.
But that's not all. He scored
down notes, war's rejoinders.

Moody teen-kissers, we wander the Towers, ignore the drug pushers, meth. dopes and narky garglers.
Scrawny lads bare-back piebald and Shetland ponies over tarmac, concrete and round the library car park.

Impossible to determine how
poems and music just begin.
She kissed him. They sensed
the peculiar revolt of things.

We stop to help little kids up abandoned car-bonnet-slides or grousing single-Mas waylaid on the stairs with grocery bags, babies, tots and double buggies. The Jaysus-crucifying lifts are down. Again.

Anna left carrying the folios.
Dmitri's seventh symphony –
shoved deep into the hidden
pockets of her coat and skirt.

A harvest moon makes us want to climb the utility ladder, try to get onto the roof of Ceannt Tower. He cradles his palms, I step in, he boosts me up, I reach and reach again. No one calls the Guards.

Pickled eggs, bread, and honey
for her journey to Tashkent.
Many places still remain
October-beautiful, not ugly.

I pull and yank down the ladder. We body-mount a safety wall. Red aircraft warning lights glare out the dark. We cuddle up, drink in our luck and sing out 'All Along the Watchtower'. The moon minds the likes of us.

Book Thieving

is easier than you think.
Line your schoolbag with tinfoil
to block the alarm sensors.
Leave textbooks in your locker.
Stuff the empty bag with loose rolls
of foolscap pages. They'll keel under
the weight of a hard-backed Sappho.

Go to Easons, alone.
Forget about a partner-in-crime.
No one minds a lone schoolgirl –
least of all a Holy Faith yonwan
in a bottle-green school uniform.
Besides, that garbardine
has a right whiff of Mary Hick.

Walk straight to the poetry section.
Wildish Things makes you stop.
Outside History translates your sighs.
Your right hand grips dull-named spines.
The left hand bags *Songs of Innocence*.
When a security man saunters your way
give him one of your bambi-eyed glances.

Lament for Collie Owens

Four hits to the chest.
Near his heart.
Two shots. Back of the head.
His face unmarked.

His mother buckled
when she heard the news.
She tried to claw
the carpet off her floor.

She got him out of Finglas,
home to her people's place.
Crossed over two rivers.
Made it to the Liberties.

She stretched him there.
Did the best she could
with his lopsided head
and wrecked ribcage.

He was safe now —
back in his Ma's bed.
Laid out on her best linen,
quiet, in his good clothes.

No words came out
of his mother's mouth.
She keened.
All. Night. Long.

Our Dublin
Pietà.
Her lullaby
gone wrong.

Flight Paths Over Finglas

We
didn't pay
that much heed
to planes, those jet streams
toing & froing at Dublin Airport.
Da taught us to keep nix, watch birds
for their covert flight paths on warm shafts
of seasonal winds and late daylight over Finglas.
The cuckoo, Hera's bird, announced each late spring.
Swifts scudded, courted above the Tolka's root-ivy summer.
Corncrakes in Darcy's side-garden scurried and secreted autumn.
Out at Dollymount, the Brent geese wing-spanned an ivory wintertime.
The finches' rise and fall – their hard flap, all that graft for a long easy glide.
We learned the most from the home place's birds. Our old feathered banner: the ravens.
How they mastered gravity vectors, omnivore feeding, prey-dodging and cloud-top scaling,
They could sense a shift in a skyscape or how a brattling rainstorm may wreck the memory map
back to the hatchling, nestling, fledgling grounds. Our ravens always returning to that magnetic place.
We heard wingbeats. Gazed up. Ravens flocked. Their sudden soaring over our estate, out beyond Finglas.

Migratory Birds

The Purple Shamrock, Boston

The manager, a Galway curlew,
tells me to swot up
on the menu
and make sure to let

the customers know
it's me first day.
I get away
with that line for weeks.

The most important thing –
feed them drink.
No one walks into an Irish pub
for the potato skins.

The cook is first generation
and roars at *her off the boat*
if I don't leg it
when his call bell ding-dings.

I glean scraps of Spanish
and get in with the Columbian
dishwashers. They got all sorts
of fingersmithin' moves.

If the INS man
walks in,
just walk out.
Do not run.

At the end of the shift
me feet are in bits.
The barman, from Cabra, hands me
a Cape Codder – cost price.

Walden Pond

Anytime we make it out,
west of Boston, to Thoreau's lake,
he tells me he's sure
he's part Native American.

We walk the cooling shadows
of the woods. Other voices rise
and echo off birch, pine and oak.
He swears it's the Nimpuc ghosts.

We're half-cut and I laugh
at my favourite descendant
of the Mayflower. His family
no more native than mine.

Still and all
I see red gashes
of earth scarred
by iron ore smelting.

I snap off a sprig
of fuchsia dog roses
and leave it
by the base of a tree.

Me fella stands still at a clearing,
happily hesitant for a chance
of frog-song, a shoal of perch –
perhaps a snapping turtle.

We yield to the cold give
of cool water between our legs.
Bask in the tingle of nipples
breast-stroking lake water.

Tucson, Arizona

The great thing about being
a babysitter for a rich family –
I get to go places I only ever saw
in the Cowboy and Indian films.

I whisper Navajo museum blurbs
to the sleeping toddler of another
woman in hope that he too might
learn something from this junket.

Pitch your tent
with a door to the east.
Rise with the sun.
Sleep with the moon.

Build a fire
to last a cold night.
Cover the embers
and cover your tracks.

Remember history
is much more than words.
It's the craft of a pot or rug
we can make and leave behind.

Gather what you want.
Hunt for what you need.
Honour the ancestors.
Papoose the young. Fur the old.

The baba stirs in his buggy.
I hip him up, like our Ma did us,
kiss him, give him raisins
and take him to change his nappy.

Emily Dickinson's Garden

The brothers think a hundred-mile road trip
to check out a dead poet's gaff is pure mad.

But I'm taken by her well-stocked herb pots,
the kitchen garden of courgette vines,
beans, potato beds with a variety of signs:
Beacon Chipper, Irish Cobbler, Castile,
White Pearl, White Rose and Yukon Gold.

It might be best to say nothing about me
smoking joints with the American fella
and sunbathing by a low hemlock hedge.
Nor will I tell a soul of the wall-eyed
ghost, in century-old clothes, who lay
the other side of me. They say she's shy.
Marya, that poet's as bold as you please.

The charm of her! She stole my *Soundings*
and read her own poems aloud, just for me.
Stony broken-mouthed, I enjoyed the trip.
Amherst, the garden, legs curled under
a white lace dress: the bride with a book.
She showed me how a little bird, a chickadee,
stored a seed into piney bark. Storm-ready.

Rice Harvest

The first day of harvest and he takes me to the family rice paddy.
We carefully walk the plank over an irrigation canal, submerge
our bare feet into silky mud and warm water. Our toes squelch.
His grandmother gives me a sun-bleached hat and new secateurs.
Together we set to work in the corners and edges of the paddy:
places he can't reach with his grandfather's harvesting machine.
The other women are deft, one chop and the stalk comes free.
They stoop, bundle, tie and fan straw out – like a girl's party dress.

I fail to get the knack of the gash so they send me off
to the drying racks. I carry wide jade stalks and hang them
from thick bamboo poles. The sun does the drying work.
Hours in the heat, rushes swish under drones of the tractor.
I run my fingers along the heavy, beady heads of kernels,
small brown pearls and long grass stems cool my sticky hands.

The women beckon me to lunch. We sit *zazen* style
under a green cherry, one mile upriver from Lake Shinji.
We lay out a picnic on tatami mats: bento boxes, fried tofu,
steamed rice, pickled veg, grilled fish and flasks of miso.
I have baked fairy cakes and tell tales of little creatures
who appear from mounds of disused bits of farm grounds
and cause all sorts of mischief in a different countryside.
He hands me a bowl of miso soup, two hands to two hands.

In a different life I could have been his wife. I might
have learned the different depths of a bow, or the language
a woman should use when she talks with an unrelated man.
I would have known how to dive deep, gather shellfish, make
a soup of aged bean and freshwater clams. He gives me food.
After the harvest, we drink. I savour the mystery of miso.

There is no Haiku in English

i.m. Emma Carroll

After a snow viewing
party, we take to hot springs
and soak in the heat.

Izimo Temple
hosts a carpet of pale pink
cheery blossom fun.

When the big rain stops
we walk dark places to catch
a glimpse of fireflies.

Bamboo paper lanterns
set sail across Lake Shinji
to honour the dead.

At his grandmother's
tea ceremony, my ring
pings her Nara cup.

He writes the kanji
for foreigner: honourable
barbaric outsider.

In a Japanese
town called Matsue,
leaves fall.

Along the river
called Liffey, leaves
fall loudly.

Forgive me, my love,
I am forgetting our once
shared language.

Family Dinner, Salpini's

Belfast, 2014

Me Ma talks
loudly

about her memory
of the bombing
in Dublin, 1974.

Me sister elbows me.

The waitress
brings us
a pot of tea,
on the house.

Mating

Samhain

Soothsayers warned I'd wed at Halloween.
Failing to fly, an owl hid me jarred broom.
You danced by with hair of a devilish sheen.
I stole your kiss under a hidden moon.
Dublin fireworks lit up the street's maisonettes.
You, me and our future edged a bonfire.
Guising ghost-kids played knick-knack-castanets
accompanied by a banshee's keen-lyre.
I felt those souls: me Da, bro and grand-folks,
crossover. Back here for the holy eve.
A witch cast love spells with whitethorn pokes.
Told me you're the one I won't want to leave.
I gave you marigolds, the harvest's rear,
as werewolves howled in our ancient new year.

Imbolig

Paper

He loves his bits of paper. His big list
for the DIY shop makes me smile –
he thinks if you buy the tool, the job is done.
His index card, Virgo instructions, set
times and temperatures for herbed vegetables,
glazed spuds and the craved marinated meat.
Don't forget, your mother has us well warned:
bad chicken might kill expectin' women.
This morning I found a PostIt in his jeans.
He must've palmed the midwife's scribbled note:
Prima-mama, 6.4 weeks – *heartbeat present.*

Cotton

The husband thinks I've gone mad for cotton.
I've given away all me polyester,
sparkly tops and frocks. The Ma helps me shop
for sheets of a fine thread count.
She swears *they'll only wash like a dream.*
Our son waddles round in sky blue muslins.
Mister has taken to pink calico
shirts and cream long-legged Irish linen.
Morning times, I go topless for breakfast
to sop up breast milk. I dress another new
baby-growing-belly in loose plain weave.
Wild fibrous boll, we are secured by cotton.

Leather

I bring his tan leather boots to the cobblers,
up by the Ma's. We've gone back to mending
everything we can. Cuts of animal
hide, teak lasts, glue, rubber and jute wafts
by as I push open Townsend's new door.
My entry chimes. I wonder who shrank
the shop, fixed old shelves, lowered the counter
and installed the bright fancy strip lighting.
The cash drawer and abacus have been ditched
for a small spacecraft of a register. But
Mr. Townsend still looks like his-same-self.
He smiles. *Tis yourself with hubby's work shoes.*
Come here, let's see. He'll be needing new heels.

Flowers

He scatters seeds of wild meadow flowers
all round the green two doors up from our gaff.
The corpo men will go feckin'mental
when they spot the latest from number 25.
They've already filed us under H, for harm-
less, but a bit loony. Even the council's
mower can't deny a couple of brazen
poppies standing guard in the corner
of a field or a scatter of soft, light
yellow primrose adoring, adorning
the trunk of the sycamore. Besides, blue
cornflowers beat ghosts of black bin bags any day.

Wood

He says he'd like to give me my own woods,
a place where I can slow-wander alone
and play a mind-bending game of hide 'n'
seek. The kids would never find me.
I'd be off, under the cover of trees,
a wife gone feral. He's no idea how
much I love the new apple blossom tree.
How much I love standing still to watch as
himself and the kids spend most of the day
digging a big deep pit to home the roots
of a sapling. It promises to bloom
each late spring and fruit every single autumn.

Iron

Iron — is what your darlin' wife won't do.
You tell the brother she's good for plenty
else but she won't go within an ass's roar
of that board behind the front room couch.
She has a knack of shakin' the wash-wet
and bejaysus out of every stitch.
She's an expert at hanging damp clothes off
banisters, kitchen chairs — even door tops.
Look, the weight of the kids' school uniforms
has them rads keeling away from the walls.
She'll fix that. Well able to handle the iron
wrench she keeps in her red tool box.

Copper

He keeps his coppers in the tall clay vase
with the broken lip. At night he empties
his pockets of ten, twenty, fifty cent
bits. Coins slide from his hand, jingle and land
onto the pile he saves daily for family
holidays, hooleys or long cold rainy days
when his Mrs. and kids want hot chocolate
with the whole mad works – fresh cream, marshmallows,
them orange popping candy chips and sprinkles.
He treats himself to a nip of whiskey.
Copper horde: soft, malleable metal coinage;
he saves and spends it all on his famo.

Ostara

Peg out your washing before you pen words.
If you have the goo for chime-rhyme, recall
the poetry of good drying weather for shirts.

Morning fog lifts while washing cauliflower curds.
Simmer a soup, add mixed spices and stall
to peg out your washing before you pen words.

Hear the kids' banter, enjoy your fella's cup of flirts,
embrace the kitchen dance of the ordinary, it scrawls
the poetry of good drying weather for shirts.

Fit in a second wash, it might sound loo-la-absurd,
but you'll sit easier at the writing table's windy squall
if you peg out your washing before you pen words.

Look, how the wind makes ash branches lurch.
Read the sky, map the day, find a way to trawl
the poetry of good drying weather for shirts.

Give the children sausi-toasties and milky smiles.
Then go, sort the mess of words into verse files.
Feck it. Find a good man, one who loves wild birds –
let him peg out your washing while you pen your words.

Bealtaine

for Paula Meehan

The car radio says
there's a horse
loose
on the Finglas Road.

I close my eyes,
recall the skewbald:
bay-brown and
white mane.

We saw her,
sinewy strong,
in the cobbler's field.
We fed her apples.

I dream us
back to Finglas.
Our Mícheál might
have a chance

to catch sight
as she breaks free
from her gnawed
tethering,

leaps
Townsend's wall
and gallops
off down the tarmac.

AA Roadwatch
advises caution.
I look at our youngest
in the rearview mirror.

He's watching YouTube,
iPhone-gazing
at the Top Ten
Horses of All Time.

Jaysus.
What would we do if
we were there
when the horse bolted?

Pull the car in,
get the child out,
perch him on the wall
to watch the show.

I need him
to witness her go.

Litha

Midsummer's Eve.
We wanna walk grass trails.
I long for me wear
in a rare Dublin field.
Come here 'til I show you,
few know about this place.

I guide you to the remnants
of our local ring fort –
a mound of grass, vetch, fern,
sticky-backs and closed buttercups.
Oak trees silhouetted in streetlight,
we're hidden and kiss like mad things.

Your tongue, our hungry mouths,
feel as gorgeous as naked plums.
You know what I'm like
and you know what I'm after.
You lift me up, skyward,
spin me and make me dizzy.

The phone pings us back
to real time in Raheny.
Our babysitter's on the clock
and tomorrow there's school.
Home to check on our two sons,
asleep in the one bed.

You load up the dishwasher.
I sweep the kitchen floor.
A late gloaming, we check
the windows and lock doors.
Outside, the garden darkens. Grows.
We go to bed and don't sleep.

Lúnasa

Listen child, they might call us slow learners
because we write b for d and can't master e.
They've yet to get – our sort are hard earners.
We make our own brainy sense, you and me.

Because we write b for d and can't master e
they send us to the resource teaching room.
We make our own brainy sense, you and me:
know how to imagine, sing and dream-zoom.

They send us to the resource teaching room
so that we can help the non-dyslexic educators
know how to imagine, sing and dream-zoom
or be better all-over-it school motivators.

So that we can help the non-dyslexic educators
enjoy a messy sequence to the days of the week.
Besides, they'd be better all-over-it school motivators
if they hide Mondays. It's Fridays students seek.

Enjoy a messy sequence to the days of the week
or confuse dates on history's repetitious timeline.
No matter, hide Mondays, it's Fridays students seek
or just an airy chance to lie still in weekend sunshine.

Go on. Question dates on history's repetitious timeline.
Don't mind the gobshites who call us slow learners.
Words work when we lie still in weekend sunshine.
People might just get it – our sort are hard earners.

Mabon

When you leave us —
I carry your migrant's kiss
like a homeless woman
carries a harvest memory
of sunshine into winter.

Working Birds

For my sisters and brothers,
Mary, Carly, Layla, Gerry, Richie, Davy, Charlo and Johnny,
as promised

The Plumber Brothers

Don't start me.
Those two can't
stop themselves.
Every gaff of ours
brings them to their knees,
their crackin' achin' knees,
for a twist and valve release
of ancient bleeding rads.
Our eldest and youngest
plumber   brothers
like to   squint out
pilot   lights,
tongue-steer
thermostats,
weigh up
ball cocks,
admire the
gush of a
second flush,
turn on and
turn off taps,
then show
every man,
woman
and child
how to shut
off gas mains
or wrench
open
water meters.

The Bricklayer

He puts his whole
body into making
the mortar
ridge and pit.

Buckets water,
edges the circle,
shovels sand,
mix-and-pitch.

He weighs
each
red brick
and checks

for fracture
left by
kiln stack
or heat-cracks.

He follows
his spirit level:
a line of twine
running along

a gravelly trough
and foundation,
pegged down
by bits of stick.

He trowels
the hawk,
slabs
the mortar,

bevels with a nifty
flick
of the hand
and wrist,

shifts to
his knees,
fixes a block
on the wall.

Pauses.
Every brick
gets a tip
of the mallet.

The Librarian

Shelving books brings him closer to paper-makers, bookbinders and typesetters.
He swears tradespeople are the only ones to put manners on them cranky writers.

Left alone, he'd throw those bewildering Dewey Decimal Classification labels out
the sash window and onto the quad's pushing-up-daisy-lawn, where they belong.

He'd create his own version of a shelving system to allow for the midnight hour
of dead Irish writers and dirty inkers to leap out of dust jackets and come alive.

Imagine James Joyce next to Samuel Beckett. Both agree not to mention L-words:
literature, love and Lucia. They'd scour desks for whiskey in hopes of a sing-song

to stop Kavanagh, Behan and O'Casey loitering with intent to get the boot into the Anglos – George Moore, Lady Gregory, Wilde and that old mystic, Yeats. Terrible beauty or wha?

The whole mob, writers and book-folk, would hush for Eibhlín Dubh Ní Chonaill as she'd keen out her blistering laments down the empty halls and echoing stacks.

In the end, the library brother assents to Dewey's ghost and shelves the books one by valued one. Outside, students lie on the lawn, kiss, dream, open books, read on.

Blood Biker

He don't get his hands
that dirty anymore.
When he was a nipper
his hands was black,
grease-monkey-manky
with bike chain oil.

He was the best lad
on our estate for fixing
sticky brakes or a slow
summer puncture.
Clunky gears did well
by that grease monkey.

He don't get his hands
that dirty anymore.
But I remember his
teenage tinkering
under the bonnets
of rust-riddled cars.

The Da handed over
Swarfega and got him
nixers from the estate.
Family and mates
said, *he's gettin' a trade,
servin' his time.*

He don't get his hands
that dirty anymore.
Has put aside his toolbox,
the ratchet, the wrench,
the combo-spanner
and bearing- puller.

He bears folders and writes
crash reports, documents
the mangle of cars,
the jaws of life,
motorway pile-ups or
unseen cyclists.

The Ma whinged on
and on as dark spills
of engine oil, coolant
or transmission fluid
seeped into concrete
and stained our drive.

He blood-bikes
twice a month, zooms
a 650, panniered
with breast milk, blood
samples, spine fluids or
bags of plasma.

He Sweenys it from
hospitals to labs.
Blue-lights it,
drives like the clappers,
swerves between cars,
leans into curves,

hugs corners
like he owns the roads,
maps out his route
via the shortcuts
only known to those born
between the canals.

He don't get his hands
that dirty anymore.
'Cept if he's needed.
When it counts,
the speed-junkie,
petrol-head comes out.

Last night, I sat
in the children's A&E,
mopping my son's
40-degree sweat
holding his hand,
anchoring him

to the bed,
begging a stop to the storm
of words: meningitis,
appendicitis,
gastroenteritis,
everything-and-anything-itis.

Unbeknownst to me,
the brother sped my child's
blood across our city
to give the doctor man a plan.
Columbanous bless
our blood-bikin' bro.

The Care Assistant

Most hoists are too big for their rooms. But she's a way to use sheets as pulleys.
Her patients are all dead weights, even the dear ones who smile encouragement through
lost teeth
seem to need
a heave-ho,
up we go.
She calls it
her early
morning
Lazarus trick.
Odds on,
Jesus never
had to shift
his old pal
onto the
HSE-issued
commode,
sponge him

You
can
bet
that
job
and
back
ache
was
left
to
the
much
put
upon
sister.

down in warm
soapy water,
to lather him
in Silcock's
Base or talc
to prevent
the dry skin
or bedsores.

Appalachian Wife

The
sister
married an
Appalachian
mountain man.
She buys dynamite
and snake-proof boots
to build a road up to her new
home. On hunkers, she bites her lip.
The safety fuse uncoils, a hiss maps out
an explosive path. A boom quarries and blasts
out boulder, rocks, topsoil, trees, weeds and moss.
My sister stands up and gives out yards to her husband.
She frets about damage to red maples, white oaks & hemlocks.
She's got the hump. He lets her stomp up-hill, the damn high road.
She pulls herself into the digger rig, glares down at her hard-hat spouse,
fires up the engine, works the levers, scoops rubble and swings 'bout the cab.
His dumper rumbles up to her. They work until blue light ridges all of Appalachia.

Teacher for the Blind

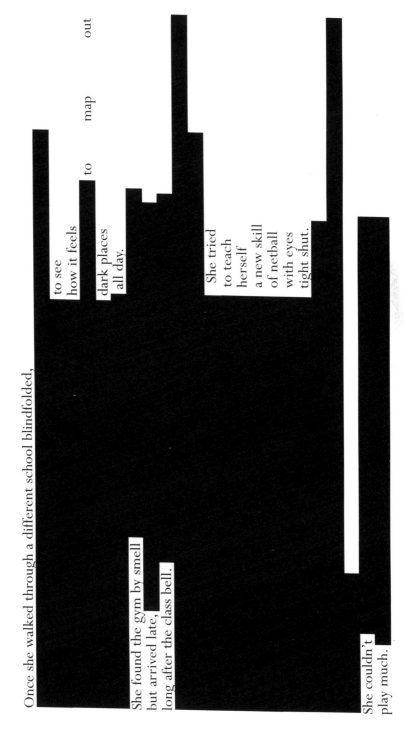

Once she walked through a different school blindfolded,

to see
how it feels

dark places
all day.

to map out

She tried
to teach
herself
a new skill
of netball
with eyes
tight shut.

She found the gym by smell
but arrived late,
long after the class bell.

She couldn't
play much.

Epilogue

You'll Nidish Find Any Minkyer On I Census

Like we'd tell that lot anything about us and ours. Gloori lackeen, the less dem know, the better it goes. Dem be wantin' lists o' names, from each raug. Names and naming be different round here. Wha' a fean's called mightn't have any bearin' to his baptisim. Dem needs exact dates and places of gawlya births — me eldest came with the roadside fushia east of here, me youngest was a daffodil west of there. Dem gadje's too curious 'bout the walking people's mass-goin', school-knowin', bloke gopin' and even lopshed. There aint no Traveller beoir'd say how many babas she bore or 'em still lucky-living. As for himself and his gruber, dem say his tinkering aint any kind of a coppering job. Dem and us thari crossways. We know other kinds of maps, places nay ever penned. I read the sky for graura and a body's palm for all its pain. You're too long in yer ken ladneach. Recall a blurt's crossroads: two sods of earth, telling her the best way to go next and to bagail only the who and what of her ukh. Light chera, grill yiesk and nap. Stop be the sheltering tree or hedge. Watch the phases of natrum moon. A road stauls you. Dili, sik families and sik people have nidish documents. Stafa tapa hum avokeen.

Nidish: no, Minkyer: Traveller, gloori lackeen: listen girl, dem: them, raug: wagon, fean: man, gawlya: child, gadje: non-Traveller, gopin: kissing, lopshed: marriage, beoir: woman, gruber: work, thari: speak, graura: summer, ken: house, ladnach: girl, blurt: a Traveller, bagail: take, ukh: need, chera: fire, yiesk: fish, nap: take off, natrum: mother, stauls: awaits, dili: daughter, sik: some, Stafa tapa hum avokeen: Long life to you loveen.

RACHAEL HEGARTY was born seventh child of a seventh child in Dublin and reared on the Northside. She was educated by the Holy Faith Sisters in Finglas, the U. Mass. Bostonians in America, the M.Phillers at Trinity and by the Ph.D. magicians at Queens. She lived, studied and worked in Boston and Japan for ten years. She is widely published in national and international journals and broadcast on RTE Radio. Rachael was the winner of the Francis Ledwidge Prize and Over the Edge New Writer of the Year. She was also shortlisted for the Hennessey New Irish Writer and Ver Poetry Prizes and highly commended for the Forward Poetry Prizes. She is an educator for the Trinity Access Programme and CDETB but reckons she learns more from her students than she can ever teach. She now lives, back on the Northside, with her feminist husband and two beloved-bedlam boys. *Flight Paths Over Finglas* was awarded the 2018 dlr Shine Strong Award for Best First Collection.

www.**salmon**poetry.com

*"Like the sea-run Steelhead salmon that thrashes upstream to its spawning
ground, then instead of dying, returns to the sea – Salmon Poetry Press
brings precious cargo to both Ireland and America in the poetry it publishes,
then carries that select work to its readership against incalculable odds."*

Tess Gallagher